I0201387

A BROKEN

A

SEARCH

تهافت "الفظي" لطلب الفاظ القرأن

A case of 'Lafzi' Apps
to search the Qoran Words

Abdul Rahman Bahry

ISBN 978-0-9892988-5-8

2 0 1 4

A BROKEN SEARCH

A case of 'Lafzi' Apps
to search the Qoran Words

© Copyright 2014, Abdul Rahman Bahry
All rights reseved

First edition 2014

No part of this book may be reproduced, stored in a
retrieval system, or transmitted by any means, electronic,
mechanical, photocopying, recording, or otherwise,
without written permission from the author.

Illustration and cover design by author

ISBN 978-0-9892988-5-8

Acknowledgment

For everyone who loves the truth

PREFACE

Can we search the Qoran words in Indonesian language? In what language and letter the Qoran is written?

'Lafzi' is a computer application to search the Qoran words; it contains a lot of mistakes and it is substandard. Since it was published in Indonesia and could be internationally accessed, it should have been pre-approved by the *Lajnah Pentashih Al-Quran* at Department of Religious Affairs of the Republic of Indonesia; but it has not.

Unfortunately, the current Secretary of *Departemen Agama RI* keeps busy with the politics and his political party more than his attention to all religious affairs even after a notification about 'Lafzi'. After having a trouble on May 22, 2014 he resigned; who would pay attention on this problem?

The Indonesian and Arabic versions of this booklet are on the way; enshaallah. The Qoran is not the Bible. The Bible is written in English and other local language; its words may be searched in Latin letters. The Qoran is written in Arabic alphabet; its words could not be searched in the Latin letters; this is biggest 'Lafzi' mistake ever. The mission of this booklet is to defend the sanctity and the glory of the Qoran. Period.

Cleveland, Ohio USA
July 22, 2013 M [Ramadan 12, 1434 H]
Revised and reviewed on May 24, 2014

Abdul Rahman Bahry
abahry@hotmail.com

TABLE of CONTENTS

1. THE QORAN and 'LAFZI' COMPUTER APPLICATION

Every scholar knows the difference between truth and false. It is possible that this book is less popular and unattractive, but it is still narrative and informative and dealing with the divine truth. This booklet is discussing the 'Lafzi' a computer application to search the words of the Qoran.

"Lafzi" with its logo لفظي at http://apps.cs.ipb.ac.id/lafzi/web/ is a computer application to search a certain word within verse(s) of the Qoran; it is a search engine alike to find a certain word in the Qoran, and displays it in full verse with translation and yellow highlight options. It would be easily named as '*Lafzi* searching tool' or 'Lafzi Search' or simply 'Lafzi' in this booklet. 'Lafzi' was designed by a student under the guidance of his supervisor at a well known Institute in West Java Indonesia. This computer application boasted the ability of *"dengan aksara Latin biasa berdasarkan pelafalan pembicara bahasa Indonesia,* **searching with input of regular Latin letter based on the pronunciation in Indonesian language**." This tag may be changed but the purpose is still the same, to search any word of the Qoran. 'Lafzi' accepts the Latin letters instead of the Arabic to search the certain verse of the Qoran. This is the **very first** and basic misrepresentation since the Qoran transliteration into any word could not exactly represent the real sound, pronunciation and meaning of the original verse of the Qoran. The writing of the Qoran word in any other letter and language other than its original Arabic is named transliteration. The word of صلاة for example, never be the same with "salat" or "shalat" or "solat" or any transliteration. From the very beginning, 'Lafzi' starts with the wrong basic thought and paradigm. The 'Lafzi' programmer and his supervisor might think that *lafaz* or words of the Qoran are like any word else. It is not true.

This booklet is based on the Qoran [Q2: 23-24] with conviction that any word in the Qoran whenever written in any language other than Arabic would alter something of its originality. Any attempt to write it in another letter and language would bring a serious consequence [Q12: 2]. Any attempt to challenge these verses would be fail, so what verse the 'Lafzi' is based on? The result of "salat" entry is a sufficient proof that 'Lafzi' is negligent and abusive to the Qoran.

The Qoran is miracle from Allah, it could not be imitated, altered, and ill-pronounced since any alteration even a very small one such as a shortened pronunciation of an elongated voice would surely change the original meaning. Try to pronounce short "na" instead of elongated "naa" of the word "f a r a q n a a' فرقنا in the Qoran [Q2:50] and take a look how far the deviation is. "Faraqnaa" with elongated aa does mean "We split [the sea for Moses and his followers]", but the shortened "na" would be translated into "the women split [their legs]". Huh? The Qoran has nothing to do with this kind of women. So, please be careful to recite, pronounce and write any *lafaz* or word of the Qoran. Moreover, the Qoran is written in Arabic, why its words should be searched in Indonesian language? Is the Qoran in Indonesian language? If the programmer and his supervisor are unable to create the computer application to search words of the Qoran in Arabic, just simply keep silence and sit nicely, since Prophet Muhammad PBUH said *"Whosoever believes in Allah and the Judgment Day, he should have said the truth or keeps silent."* The prophet also said *"Whosoever said any false about me, he should take his stand in the Fire."* This is the religious decree.

Now, for the 'Lafzi' programmer and his supervisor, what is their original religious decree from the Qoran and Hadis about creating the defective 'Lafzi' which considered and found 'RISALAT' as a result of searching 'SALAT' entry? They do not have to answer now, answer to Allah in the Judgment Day! Is this not enough for them to voluntarily stop and recall 'Lafzi'?

The Qoran is not just about pronunciation in Indonesian language or *'pelafalan pembicara bahasa Indonesia'*, the Qoran is about the Miraculous Sripture originated from Allah revealed through Gabriel the Angel to the Last Messenger Phrophet Muhammad PBUH as is, and never changed ever since. It is not jut 'lafaz', it is not just the word, it is miracle. Let us realize this basis first before anything else about the Qoran. After several attempts to find the certain verses of the Qoran, some irregularities were found. The Qoran verses in this booklet were *not always* fully displayed and quoted for reason, some verses were rewritten based on the original Qoran, and some of them just simply quoted with Surah name and verse number. Both the student who designed 'Lafzi' and his supervisor did not have the sufficient formal education in Arabic Language, Arabic Literature and the Qoran study.

They had crossed the academic line by discussing and making the special computer application pertaining to the Quran which is beyond their academic capacities and capabilities.

'Lafzi' is kind of arrogance of unknowledgeable person who pretends to be knowledgeable. Do they think that they would be welcomed as the heroes since *they have the ability to make computer program* related to the Qoran **without** studying the Qoran sciences? Their expertise in the computer programming and other secular sciences are not enough to help them creating the sufficient computer application about the Qoran words. Therefore, the end result of their efforts was filled up with structural and logical mistakes and afar from the Qoran standard which was preserved in the high level Arabic language and memorized by millions of Muslim, and written in the clear and standardized Arabic as well since more than 1,400 year ago. The next Chapters would refute 'Lafzi' and explain the proofs that 'Lafzi' is a big mistake.

The nomenclature of standard Arabic language is very specific; it did not change since more than 14 centuries ago; in Arabic we know the *Kalam* (sentence), *lafadz* (word), *isim* (noun), *Fi'l* (verb) and *harf* (functioning letter). This is the basic and foundation of Arabic language. The 'Lafzi' application has failed to identify them all and resulted in a lot of serious mistakes. The 'Lafzi' has failed in searching several words or 'lafaz', especially:

The Clear Mistake in searching Simple single Noun or phrase (الإسـم والاسماء)
The Clear Mistake in searching Adjective (الصـفة)
The Clear Mistake in searching Present Tense Verb (فعل المـضـارع)
The Clear Mistake in searching Past Tense Verb (فعل ماض)
The Clear Mistake in searching Imperative Verb (فعل امـر)
The Clear Mistake in searching Authoritative Verb (فعل نهـي)
The Clear Mistake in searching Multiple Noun (مضـاف مضـاف إليه)
The Clear Mistake in searching Objective Noun (مفعـول به)
The Clear Mistake in searching Seasonal Objective Noun (مفعـول مـعه)
The Clear Mistake in searching Noun with Relative Pronoun (أسـم وضـمير)

Let us make clear once more time, the Qoran is not just the word or 'lafaz', it is the Divine Miracle, a whole or a part of it is still miracle.

2. SEARCHING WORD of 'SALAT'

"Salat."

When the Arabic word of "salat" that does mean "pray" or "prayer" was entered to 'Lafzi' computer application, the result(s) is 185 entries:

> "Hasil Pencarian (185 hasil)"

2.1. Some results out of 185 even are NOT connected at all with the "salat" or "shalat" entry which means pray or prayer. The worst result is, the 'Lafzi' displays the word of RISALAT just because this word contains the sound or Latin letter of S-A-L-A-T. The word of "RISALAT" in Surah Al-A'raf verse # 62 does mean "COMMANDs;" and "MURSALAT" in Surah Al-Mursalat verse #1 does mean "commanded Angels." 'Lafzi' clearly displayed some results which are not related at all to "prayer." This result is absolutely biased since the primary target is searching "salat" or prayer; instead it displays "Commands, etc." From the stand point of scientific standard, it is questionable.

2.2. From the point of the linguistic, the entry 'salat' is *'Isim nakirah mufrad muannaš* or singular masculine indefinite noun' but the **'risalat'** result is the noun in the category of *'Jamak mu'anaš-Salim* or the regular plural masculine noun;' a significant deviation in the strict rule of the Qoran language since the meaning has been altered too far. It is unacceptable from the point of linguistic and the religious standard.

2.3. There are still another 5 (five) biases of the 'salat' entry with the result of 'RISALAT:' رسَالَاتِ Surah Al-A'raf (7:62), رسَالَاتِ Surah Al-A'raf (7:68), رسَالَاتِ Surah Al-Jin (72:28), وَالْمُرْسَلَاتِ Surah Al-Mursalat (77:1), رِسَالَّةَ Surah Al-An'am (6:124). Why do we search "salat" (= prayer) and find "risalat" (= commands), "mursalat" (commanded Angels) etc? Does it make sense?

---

3. SEARCHING WORD of 'SHALAT'

"Shalat."

Let us try another entry. When the Arabic word of "shalat" that does mean "pray" or "prayer" was entered to 'Lafzi'; it does not have any the result. It displays:

> **Hasil Pencarian (0 hasil)**
> Tidak ada hasil. Pastikan lafaz yang dicari adalah lafaz pada Al-Quran.

Result (0) No result. Make sure the word you are searching is the Qoran word

The ص 14th letter of Arabic Alphabet used to be transliterated into "sh" in Indonesian; while in the other system "sh" represent ش the 13th Arabic Aphabet.

The big question; is it right that no word of "shalat" or صلاة in the Qoran entirely? This computer application was NOT designed to accept the Arabic letter, but the entry with Latin or common letter brings so many mistakes. It is absolutely not right that no such word in the Qoran, the plausible explanation is the programmer does not have the sufficient knowledge about the Qoran words.

The Qoran printed in Damascus, Syria, 1987

4. THE WORD of 'SOLAT'

"Solat."

Since 'Lafzi' does not find the result of "shalat" entry, let us try another entry, "solat" which still has the same meaning of "pray or prayer". The result is even worst; especially result # 32, 33, 35, and 36.

4.1.   The result #32; Surah An-Nahl (16:74),

فَلَا تَضْرِبُوا لِلَّهِ الْأَمْثَالَ

The result sounds "**LA –T**adhribuu" that does mean "do not take a parable of;" it comes to this result just because this phrase contains the sound of "LA-T," similar to the last part of "soLAT"; this is the most weird result ever.

The programmer is so negligent to the Qoran verse. He did not know what to do; he is not eligible to discuss the Qoran in such a way. The "LA-T" in this result actually consists of two different words "La" and "Tadhribu." The pronunciation of these two words are always with elongation "Laa", if "Laa Tadhribu" is pronounced directly becomes "Latadhribu" and then the original meaning has been altered, and it is a major mistake according to the *Tajwid* and *Tawhid* sciences. Why did the programmer make the application that leads him to the significant sin according to Islam? The danger and loss are much more than its benefit; according to the *Ushul-Fiqh* it is absolutely not permissible.

Is "LA-T" included in the result of "solat?" It is totally unacceptable from the point of linguistic and religious value. From the ***Nahwu*** science, "Laa Tadhribu" consists of a prohibition letter "Laa" which is commonly known as "*Laa an-Nahyi*", and "Tadhribu" an *authoritative verb* or "***Fi'l Nahyi majzum***" which is originated from a present tense verb and intended to prohibit of doing something. How come the entry "solat" or prayer has strayed to this result? It happens only if the programmer or his supervisor is unknowledgeable.

Tajwid, Nahwu and *Sorf* sciences clearly and strictly forbid the combination of long "Laa" with the adjacent verb by cutting the elongation off to be "LaT....." Neither the programmer nor the supervisor knew this strict rule in the Quran science. By combining "Laa" and "T...." the original meaning has been lost, how dare the unknowledgeable programmer and his supervisor decided to release "Lafzi" to the community without proper knowledge of *Tajwid, Nahwu, Sorf, Badi', Ma'any* and *Bayan* sciences. Their major of study is around "farming" or "botany" or "computer science" or something like that or another secular science, and not directly related to the Qoran science at all. The Qoran is not their expertise.

4.2. Result #33: Surah Al-Mu'min (40:8)

الَّتِي وَعَدْتَهُمْ

The result sounds "al**LAT**ii" it does mean "which." The result is "allatii" a conjunction or *mausul*, and not "solat" in the form of *'isim nakirah mufrad muannaš* or singular masculine indefinite noun.' Just because it has sound of "LAT" and then it was considered and displayed as an output.

4.3. Result #35: Surah Al-Baqarah (2:196)

ثَلَاثَةٍ and وَلَا تَحْلِقُوا رُءُوسَكُمْ

The result has a double jeopardy, the *first* sounds "LA-T" in combination of the first and second adjacent words of "Laa" and "Tahliquu" that means 'do not shave.' The *second* sounds T**SALAT**S means **'three'**. In the entire Quran, there is never be the word that sounds "**Lat**ahliqu" with short 'a' on 'Laa.' The correct pronunciation of this *lafaz* is "Laa-Tahliquu", "Laa" with *madd* or, *elongation*, or extended. The explanation is similar to aforementioned in point 4.1.

The second jeopardy is even worst. The "solat" entry never contained any pronunciation or *pelafalan* of 'š' or 'Ts' ث the fourth letter of Arabic alphabet/Hejai. We are searching صلاة which contains the pronunciation of the ص the fourteenth letter of Arabic Hejai, and NOT the ث fourth letter. This mistake is really disgusting. Does the 'Lafzi' programmer know the diference between 14th and 4th?

4.4. Result #36: Surah An-Nisa' (4:22)

--- وَلَا تَنْكِحُوا مَا نَكَحَ آبَاؤُكُم

The result sounds "**Laa T**ankihuu" a combination of first and second word sounds like "LAT" the very same mistake as aforementioned in 4.1 and 4.3.

The programmer and supervisor have made the very same mistake 3 (three) times, while the proverb says 'Even the d@&#*% does not make two same mistakes.'

The Most popular English translation of the Qoran,
by Abdullah Yusuf Ali

5. SEARCHING WORD of 'INNA SALATAKA'

'Salat, inna salataka"

The aforementioned mistakes were obtained from http://apps.cs.ipb.ac.id/lafzi/web/ between July 13 and July 14, 2013; and 'Lafzi' could be reprogrammed afterwards since the subject was discussed on the internet mail list as described in the Appendices. On Tuesday July 16, 2013 'Lafzi' was used once more time; the entry was "**salat**". Astonishingly, the result was not similar to the previous one as described in point 2.1 – 2.3. The result was:

> *"Berikanlah masukan yang lebih panjang agar hasil lebih akurat. Pencarian dalam 0.01 detik"*

Please enter longer entry for more accuracy. Search in 0.001 second

We knew that the result of previous search with the very same entry of '**salat**' was "**Hasil Pencarian (185 hasil).**" It had 185 results. Now, it has no result at all, even with a weird instruction to put *more entry for accuracy.* The '**Lafzi**' instruction to add more entry; and its incapability to accept a single word input indicating its basic flaw, and at the same time indicating that the programmer and his supervisor do not have a sufficient knowledge about the Qoran words.

To complying with the computer instruction to enter a longer entry; it was typed "**inna salataka**" (= *verily your prayer*), and the result is 1 correct result, plus *3 almost right results*, and bonus of 25 inaccurate results. The list of inaccuracy would be longer whenever output of "as-**salata**" and "in**nas-salata**" in Surah An-Nisa' (4:103); and "**salli**" in Surah At-Taubah (9:103) are considered inaccurate since the computer clearly asked the longer entry and it is the specific "**inna salataka**", and nothing else. The one and only correct result of "**inna salataka**" is in the beginning of the verse of (Q9:103).

The search of "inna salataka" has resulted 6 verses with at least 25 inaccuracies; they are not the mistakes of the Qoran, but the Lafzi's:
(1) Surah Al-Baqarah (2:228)

(2) Surah Al-Isra' (17:36)
(3) Surah Al-Isra' (17:36)
(4) Surah Al-Ahqaaf (46:15)
(5) Surah At-Taubah (9:103)
(6) Surah Yusuf (12:31).

5.1.   Surah Al-Baqarah (2:228)

وَالْمُطَلَّقَاتُ يَتَرَبَّصْنَ بِأَنْفُسِهِنَّ ثَلَاثَةَ قُرُوءٍ
وَبُعُولَتُهُنَّ أَحَقُّ بِرَدِّهِنَّ

The 'Lafzi' result has 5 (five) mistakes:

5.1.1.   "Al-Mutallaqaatu" الْمُطَلَّقَاتُ was considered as a result of searching **"inna salataka"** just because it contains a partial sound of **"la"**, while this word has a meaning of "the divorced women" not "verily your prayer" as intended in the entry of **"inna salataka"**.

5.1.2.   "Yatarabbashna" يَتَرَبَّصْنَ was considered as a result of searching **"inna salataka"** just because it contains a partial sound of **"ta"**, while this word has a meaning of "they wait" or *they should wait for a certain period to remarry*. This word clearly does not have the meaning of "verily your prayer" as intended in the entry of **"inna salataka"**.

5.1.3.   "Bi-anfusihinna" بِأَنْفُسِهِنَّ was considered as a result of searching **"inna salataka"** just because it contains a partial sound of **"nna"**, while this word has a meaning of "by themselves" not "verily your prayer" as intended in the entry of **"inna salataka"**.

5.1.4.   "Tsalatsata" ثَلَاثَةَ was considered as a result of searching **"inna salataka"** just because it contains a partial sound of **"la"** and **"ta"** while this word has a meaning of "three" not "verily your prayer" as intended in the entry of **"inna salataka"**.

5.1.5. "Wa bu'ulatuhunna" وَبُعُولَتُهُنَّ was considered as a result of searching **"inna salataka"** just because it contains a partial sound of "lat", while this word has a meaning of "their husbands" not "verily your prayer" as intended in the entry of **"inna salataka"**.

5.2. Surah Al-Isra' (17:36)

وَلَا تَقْفُ مَا لَيْسَ لَكَ بِهِ عِلْمٌ إِنَّ السَّمْعَ ـــــــــ

In this result, 'Lafzi' has 3 mistakes:

5.2.1. "**Laa**" لَا was considered as a result of searching **"inna salataka"** just because it contains a partial sound of "la", while this word has a meaning of "No" or "Do not", it is not "verily your prayer" as intended in the entry of **"inna salataka"**.

5.2.2. "**Laysa laka**" لَيْسَ لَكَ was considered as a result of searching **"inna salataka"** just because it contains a partial sound of "la" and "ka", while this word has a meaning of "for you" not "verily your prayer" as intended in the entry of **"inna salataka"**.

5.2.3. "**Inna** as-Sam'a" إِنَّ السَّمْعَ was considered as a result of searching **"inna salataka"** just because it contains a partial sound of "**inna**" this word has a meaning of "verily" only a part of long entry "verily your prayer" as intended in **"inna salataka"**. Whenever "inna" is considered as a correct result, why does the computer application ask for longer entry at the beginning? Well, this result may be considered as one half correct.

5.3. Surah An-Nisa' (4:103)

فَإِذَا قَضَيْتُمُ الصَّلَاةَ ـــــ إِنَّ الصَّلَاةَ

In this result, 'Lafzi' contains 2 almost correct results:

5.3.1. "Fa idza qodhoitum" فَإِذَا قَضَيْتُمُ
This phrase became the searching result of **"inna salataka"** maybe because it contains the word of "as-salata."

5.3.2. "As-Shalata" الصَّلَاةَ is *"isim ma'rifah muannaŝ"* or the feminine definite noun; even though it does have a partial correct result, but the phrase of **"inna salataka"** consists of *"tarkib idhofi"* or multiple noun a combination of noun and relative pronoun or *"dhomir"*. Result does not match the intended multiple entry of **"inna salataka"**. The detail of multiple-entry is absolutely unknown by the computer programmer and his supervisor, and this structural detail of the Quran word never be recognized by those who never specifically learn the Arabic linguistic, Arabic literature and the Quran science. Therefore, the computer programmer and his supervisor do not have the competency and authority to distribute the flaw 'Lafzi' application.

5.4. Surah Al-Ahqaaf (46:15)

وَوَصَّيْنَا الْإِنْسَانَ بِوَالِدَيْهِ إِحْسَانًا حَمَلَتْهُ أُمُّهُ كُرْهًا وَوَضَعَتْهُ كُرْهًا ----

The 'Lafzi' result contains 9 (nine) mistakes, this is the worst ever, even after the programmer' supervisor received the notification through email which enclosed in the Appendices. They went astray and this time is too very so far:

5.4.1. "Wa waŝŝaina" وَوَصَّيْنَا was considered as a result of searching **"inna salataka"** just because it contains a partial sound of "ŝa" while this word has a meaning of "and We ordained" it is not "verily your prayer" as intended in **"inna salataka"**.

5.4.2. "Al-<u>Insaana</u>" was considered as a result just because it contains the sounds of "**in**", "**sa**" and "**na**" as a part of **"<u>in</u> <u>na</u> <u>sa</u>lataka"** while "Al-<u>Insaana</u>" does mean "the

12

human being" it is not "verily your prayer" as intended in **"inna salataka"**.

5.4.3. "Hama**lat**-hu" حَمَلَتْهُ was considered as a result just because it contains a sounds of "**lat**" as a part of **"inna salataka"** while "Hamalat-hu" does mean "she conceived him" it is not "verily your prayer" as intended in **"inna salataka"**.

5.4.4. "Fi**ṣa**luhu" فِصَالُهُ was considered as a result just because it contains a sound of "**ṣa**" as a part of **"inna ṣalataka"** while "Fiṣaluhu" does mean "separation from breast feeding" it is not "verily your prayer" as intended in **"inna salataka"**.

5.4.5. "Tsalat**sun**a" ثَلاثُونَ was considered as a result just because it contains the sounds of "**tsalat**" and "**na**" as a part of **"inna salatuna"** while "Tsalatsuna" has meaning of "thirty" and not "verily your prayer" as intended in **"inna salataka"**.

5.4.6. "Syahron" or "ṣahron" شَهْرًا. It is pretty difficult to explain on why this is included as a search result. 'Lafzi' originally highlight the ش first letter with yellow color indicating that this letter is considered as a part of sounds in **"inna salataka"**. For your information, the ش letter is the 13th letter of Arabic Hejai while the letter of ص is the 14th letter of Arabic Hejai. This mistake is very embarrassing, the computer programmer and his supervisor do not even know the *Alif Ba Ta'* in Arabic Hejai which the Qoran was written in; they crossed the academic demarcation line, from the "farming or botany or computer or something like that discipline" to the Qoran science where they know nothing but the wrong guess. *Wal-'iyadzu billah.* OMG.

5.4.7. "Hatta" حَتَّى This word is a conjunction in Arabic, and it has 2 "ta" sounds or bold "ta". It was considered as a result just because it contains the sounds of "**ta**" as a part of **"inna salataka"** while "Hatta" has meaning of "until" and not "verily your prayer" as intended in **"inna salataka"**.

5.4.8. "Arbai'**ina**" أَرْبَعِينَ was considered as a result just because it contains the sound of "**na**" as a part of **"inna salataka"**. "Arbai'ina" has meaning of "forty" and not "verily your prayer" as intended in **"inna salataka"**.

5.4.9. "Ni'ma**taka**" نِعْمَتَّك was considered as a result just because it contains the sound of "**taka**" as a part of **"inna salataka"**. "Ni'ma**taka**" has meaning of "Your blessing" and not "verily your prayer" as intended in **"inna salataka"**.

5.5. Surah At-Taubah (9:103)

خُذْ مِنْ أَمْوَالِهِمْ صَدَقَةً تُطَهِّرُهُمْ وَتُزَكِّيهِمْ بِهَا وَصَلِّ عَلَيْهِم ---

'Lafzi' considered this verse is one of the search results of entry **"inna salataka"**. 'Lafzi' has one and only correct; one almost correct and one wrong result:

5.5.1. "Shadaqo**tan**" صَدَقَةً It is pretty hard to explain on why this is included as a searsh result. 'Lafzi' originally highlight the ة letter with yellow color indicating that this letter is considered as a part of sounds or pronunciations in **"inna salataka"**. For your information, the ة letter is pronounced "**tan**" not "**ta**" in this verse. This letter is a wrapped (*marbutah*) version of the 3rd letter of Arabic Hejai. Are the computer programmer and his supervisor smart enough to know the '*Alif Ba Ta*' in Arabic Alphabet?

5.5.2. "Shalli" صَلِّ This result is almost correct since it contains the ص "**ṣa**" and ل "**lam**" letters, they are two among original letters in the Qoran text. However, the result has missed the multiple noun and relative pronoun as the original entry contained. This "Shalli" does mean "pray" an imperative while the entry is *verily your prayer* "**inna salataka**".

5.5.3. "Inna salataka" إِنَّ صَلَاتَكَ There you go! This is so far the one and only correct result of entry search. *Allah Akbar, alhamdu lillah.*

5.6. Surah Yusuf (12:31)

فَلَمَّا سَمِعَتْ بِمَكْرِهِنَّ أَرْسَلَتْ إِلَيْهِنَّ وَأَعْتَدَتْ لَهُنَّ مُتَّكَأً وَآتَتْ كُلَّ وَاحِدَةٍ مِنْهُنَّ سِكِّينًا...

In this result, 'Lafzi' has another 8 (eight) mistakes, it is the second record after 9 mistakes as explained in 5.4.:

5.6.1. "Fa**la**mma" فَلَمَّا was considered as a result just because it contains the sound of "**la**" as a part of "**inna salataka**". "Fa**la**mma" has meaning of "As for" and not "verily your prayer" as intended in "**inna salataka**".

5.6.2. "**Sa**mi'at" سَمِعَتْ was also considered as a result just because it contains the sound of "**sa**" as a part of "**inna salataka**". "Sami'at" does mean "she heard" and not "verily your prayer" as intended in "**inna salataka**".

5.6.3. "Bimakrih**inna**" بِمَكْرِهِنَّ This phrase was considered as a result just because it contains the sound of "**inna**" as a part of "**inna salataka**". **Actually the sound of "inna" within** "Bimakrih**inna**" is a fraction of *dhamir* or Arabic relative pronoun "**hinna**"; and does not stand alone as "inna". "Bimakrih**inna**" has the meaning of "of their plot, or their gossip" and not "verily your prayer" as intended in "**inna salataka**". The programmer and his supervisor are now totally helpless.

5.6.4. "Ar**salat**" أَرْسَلَتْ It is pretty difficult to explain on why this is included as a searsh result. 'Lafzi' originally highlight 3 letters سَلَتْ ت ل س which is pronounced 'salat' with a yellow color indicating that these 3 letters are considered as the part of sounds in "**inna salataka**".

Here is the explanation of the mistake(s):

(a) For the information, the س letter is the 12ᵗʰ letter of Arabic Alphabet or Hejai while the letter of ص is the 14ᵗʰ letter. This mistake is very awkward, the computer programmer and his supervisor for several times do not even know the '*Alif Ba Ta*' in Arabic Hejai which the Qoran was written in. *Wal-'iyadzu billah.* OMG.

(b) 'Lafzi' considered the phrase of "Ar<u>salat</u>" أَرْسَلَتْ as the search result of entry **"inna <u>salataka</u>"** just because it contains sounds "*salat*"; while actually it is a fraction of "*arsalat*" and not real pronunciantion or *pelafalan* of صلاة "salat". "Ar<u>salat</u>" أَرْسَلَتْ does mean *"she sent the invitation or she invited"*. We are serching **"inna <u>salataka</u>"** (verily your prayer), not *'she invited'*.

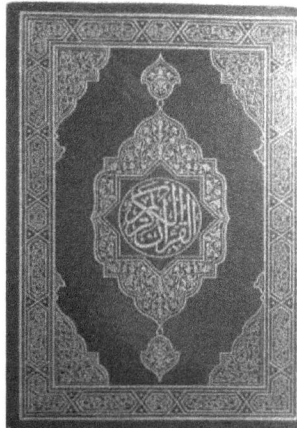

King Fahd of Saudi Arabia ordered to print millions of the Qoran and distributed to the Muslim World for free. *Allah yarham; May Allah Bless his soul.*

(c) From the stand point of *Nahwu* or Arabic Linguistic, "**arsalat**" is *fi'l-madhi mufrad muannaš* or *past tense verb for a lady* where the sound of "**s**" originated from س the 12th letter in Arabic Alphabet/Hejai, while "**s**" sound within the entry "**inna Salataka**" originated from ص the 14th letter in Arabic Hejai. "Ar**salat**" أَرْسَلَتْ is the <u>verb</u> and صلاة is the <u>noun</u>, either meaning or nomenclature do not match at all. The Qoran has meticulous and accurate way to express any meaning in a word; it is not just a word, it is a Divive Word. The 'Lafzi' programmer and his supervisor do not even know the difference between **verb** and **noun** in the Qoran *lafaz*. OMG!

Is this the computer program intended to search the words in the Qoran? Are the computer programmer and his supervisor the experts in the Qoran linguistic? Does their famous alma mater to approve the computer application named 'Lafzi'? Do they realize that they violate the glory of the Qoran? This 'Lafzi' has gone astray and had the possibility to lead the Muslims going astray.

5.6.5. "Mutta**ka**'an" مُتَّكَأً was considered as a result just because it contains the sound of "**ka**" as a part of "**inna salataka**". "Mutta**ka**'an" مُتَّكَأً does mean "chair" or something to sit on, and not "verily your prayer" as intended in "**inna salataka**". From the stand point of the Qoran Linguistic, the sound of "**ka**" is actually a fraction of "Mutta**ka**'an" the *isim nakirah manshub* or *indefinite article or noun as object* (*maf'ul-bih*) while "**ka**" within the entry "**inna salataka**" is a relative pronoun or *dhomir* in the position of ضميرومضاف إليه وهومجرورمبني علي الفتح or *defensive multiple noun but should be firmly pronounced as objective*. The letter of ك should have been pronounced "ke" yet it could not be changed from original "ka" since the meaning would be badly altered. This is a miracle among tons of miracles of the Qoran even in every single letter in a word which is never be recognized by the 'Lafzi' programmer and his supervisor. Their multiple mistakes indicated that they are absolutely unknowledgeable and ineligible to deal with the words of the Qoran. They are ignorant of the Qoran but acted as if they are experts.

5.6.6. "Aa**tat**" آتَت was considered as a result just because it contains the sound of "**ta**" as a part of **"inna salataka"**. "Aa**tat**" آتَت has a meaning of "she provided", and not "verily your prayer" as intended in **"inna salataka"**. The sound or voice or pronunciation of "**ta**" is actually a fraction of "aa**tat**" a past tense verb or *fi'l-madhi muannaš mabny* while "**ta**" of the entry is the fraction of "**salata**" an objective noun within a multiple composition or *isim manshub mudhof* within "**inna salataka**". The result does not conform the entry neither its meaning nor nomenclature. This serious mistake has denigrated the glory of the Qoran. This computer application has to be discarded immediately, either voluntarily or forcibly by the court ruling to save the Muslims from being misguided. The computer programmer and his supervisor do not know the difference between the **verb** and the **noun** in the Qoran; how come the ignorant of the Qoran to guide the Muslim nation? Their expertise in the computer science is absolutely insufficient at all to create an appropriate computer application to search the words of the Qoran.

5.6.7. "Minhu**nna**" مِنْهُنَّ was considered as a result just because it contains the sound of "**nna**" as a part of "**inna** salataka". "Minhu**nna**" مِنْهُنَّ does mean "among them", and not "verily your prayer" as intended in **"inna salataka"**. The sound or pronunciation of "**nna**" comes from "**hunna**" (them). Either "**Hunna**" or "**ka**" is Arabic relative pronoun or *dhomir* but with a clear difference between the both. "Hunna" refers to "them" (three or more ladies) while "ka" refers to "your" (one man).

From this point, it is doubtful that 'Lafzi' is the scientific output or scientific product or scientific paperwork as the one among academic requirements to reach an academic degree since both its programmer and his supervisor do not have the scientific knowledge pertaining to the Qoran words and do not even know the relative pronoun in the Qoran where their subject is concerned about.

5.6.8. "In" إنْ was also considered as a result just because it contains the sound of "**in**" as a part of **"inna salataka"**. "In" إنْ does mean "nothing", and not "verily your prayer" as intended in **"inna salataka"**. The إنْ "**in**" and ما "**maa**" are letters to construct the special composition which is popular with the name of "*tarkib istišna*" or "*harfu-nafy – istišna – mustašna*" in the Arabic *Nahwu*. This linguistic composition is pretty complicated which is recognized only by those who learned the Arabic Linguistic and Arabic Literature. The "*tarkib istišna*" contains at least 2 (two) basic rules:

(a) When it is dealing with noun and verb (*isim* wa *fi'il*) on when a *mustašna* should be pronounced *rafa'* (**o** vowel) or when it should be pronounced *našab* (**a** vowel).

(b) When it is dealing with a verbal sentence or جملة فعلية on how a verb may be exempted from following the masculine and feminine classification of subject.

In this particular case, Imam Muhammad bin Malik explained in his famous book "*Alfiyyah*":

والحذف مع فصل بإلا فضلا   *   كمـا زكـا إلا فتـاة ابـن العـلا

*The omission of feminine sign [in a verb] is preferable whenever a feminine subject and its verb are separated with "ella" (= but) as described in this example '**Maa zaka ella fataat'**

Normally, the verb matches up with the subject in gender; if a subject is feminine the verb has to be feminine. Do the 'Lafzi' programmer and his supervisor know this very specific linguistic rule in the Qoran? No wonder that 'Lafzi' is filled up with so many mistakes!

The *"tarkib istišna"* or "no – subject – but" package is a very specific composition which becomes a part of the Qoran miracles; on this composition the *shahada "I bear witness that no God but Allah"* or Islamic creed is composed on. This is a miracle among tons of miracles of the Qoran which is nobody able to imitate since more than 1,400 years ago.

The Qoran challenged everybody **"If you are in doubt about anything we revealed to Our Servant (Muhammad PBUH), and then bring forward a chapter similar to the Qoran, and call all your witnesses except Allah; if you are truthful"** [Q2:23]. Nobody answered this perpetual challenge since 1,435 years ago even until the Doomsday. Is 'Lafzi' trying to answer this challenge?

Both computer programmer and his supervisor might be educated in the computer science or farming or botany, but they never academically obtained the formal education in the Quran science and the relevant sciences such as *Nahwu, Sorf, Bayan, Ma'any, Badi', Tajweed*, etc. The 'Lafzi' computer application is a suicide mission alike; any publication pertaining to the Qoran text should have obtained the pre-approval from Department of Religious Affairs 'Departemen Agama RI'. They neglected the rule and are ignorant of the Qoran yet acted as if they are the experts. Is it acceptable?

By statistics, 'Lafzi' found only 1 correct result compared to 27 mistakes; 1:27 = 3.7%. This tiny prevalence does not meet requirement to be valid result in a research. Any sane scientist would reject this kind of result as scientific; therefore 'Lafzi' has to be rejected; it is false and broken tool to search *lafaz* or word in the Qoran.

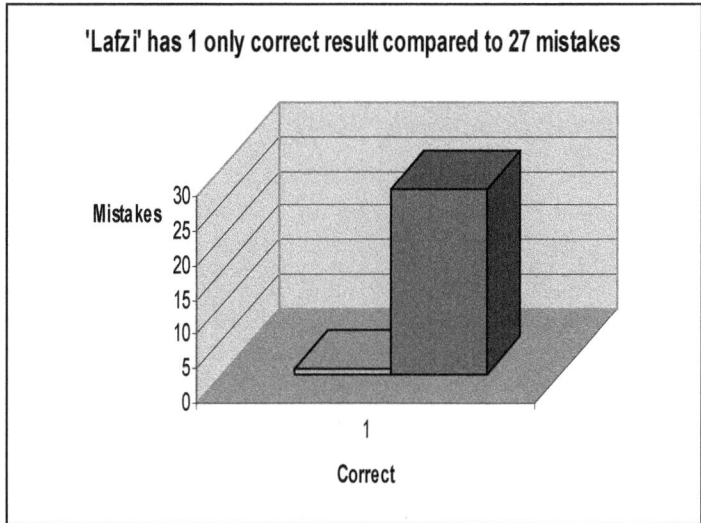

'Lafzi' has 1 only correct result compared to 27 mistakes

Mistakes

30
25
20
15
10
5
0

1

Correct

They can not hide behind the academic freedom or any reason to violate and denigrate the Muslim Scripture. The effort to have 'Lafzi' fixed would be an obligation for the sake of Allah. The email address is clearly written in this booklet to make everyone feel comfortable to discuss or ask anything related to the main topic. We should have been very careful to use http://apps.cs.ipb.ac.id/lafzi/web/. If it could not be fixed, or the programmer and his supervisor are unable to fix it or if they deny fixing it for any reason, and then any legal effort to eradicate it becomes obligatory, we will it do at any cost.

6. THE WORD of "LAA TA'MANNAA"

Word of "laa ta'mannaa" لاتأمنا

On July 21, 2013 the other mistake was found. It is possible that 'Lafzi' has been fixed; however there are still some mistakes found. This time the entry is a phrase (not a single word) as suggested by the supervisor of this computer application through his email to the author. The phrase is Arabic **"laa ta'mannaa"** (= *why don't you trust us?*). The result is "significant", 1 correct result plus bonus of 7 (seven) mistakes. By statistics it is 1:7 or 14.28% a very low result.

The search result of **"laa ta'mannaa"** entry would be better and more accurate whenever the computer programmer and his supervisor learn and understand well the rule of *tilawah* within the *Tajwid* science. Why? Because according to the *Tajwid* there is one and only kind of *Işmam* pronunciation i.e. **"laa ta'mannaa"** phrase in the whole Qoran, in Surah Yusuf [**Q12:11**]. 'Lafzi' should have stopped searching after finding **"laa ta'mannaa"** in Surah Yusuf since it is the one and only result in the whole Qoran, nothing else! The further search would be definitely failed. This is very distinctive *Işmam* pronunciation which both the 'Lafzi' programmer and his supervisor never knew! Do they think that the Qoran just a b c pronunciation and transliteration?

A beautiful cover of the Qoran

7. THE NUMBER of 'SALAT' WORD

Word of "Salat" in Number

The truth is; there are more than 69 words or lafaz of "salat" or "shalat" or صلاة within entire the Qoran, the number would be more whenever we count the derivative words:

9 words of "salat" in Surah Al-Baqarah
9 words of "salat" in Surah An-Nisa'
6 words of "salat" in Surah Al-Ma'idah
1 word of "salat" in Surah Al-An'am
1 word of "salat" in Surah Al-A'raf
1 word of "salat" in Surah Al-Anfal
5 words of "salat" in Surah At-Tawbah
1 word of "salat" in Surah Yunus
1 word of "salat" in Surah Huud
1 word of "salat" in Surah Ar-Ra'd
3 words of "salat" in Surah Ibrahim
1 word of "salat" in Surah Al-Isra'
3 words of "salat" in Surah Maryam
2 words of "salat" in Surah Taha
1 word of "salat" in Surah Al-Anbiya'
3 words of "salat" in Surah Al-Hajj
4 words of "salat" in Surah An-Nuur
1 word of "salat" in Surah An-Naml
2 words of "salat" in Surah Al-'Ankabuut
1 word of "salat" in Surah Ar-Ruum
2 words of "salat" in Surah Luqman
1 word of "salat" in Surah Al-Ahzaab
2 words of "salat" in Surah Faathir
1 word of "salat" in Surah As-Shuuraa
1 word of "salat" in Surah Al-Mujaadalah
1 word of "salat" in Surah Al-Jumu'ah
1 word of "salat" in Surah Al-Muzzammil
1 word of "salat" in Surah Al-Bayyinah
1 word "inna **salat**aka" in Surah At-Tawbah
1 word "a**salat**uka" in Surah Huud
1 word "bi**salat**ika" in Surah Al-Isra'

These are 69 words or lafaz of "salat", the *derivative and morph* words such as "salatu-ka", "salata-hu", "salata-hum", "salati-him", "salati, "salawat", "salluu", "yusalluuna" etc. are not included; and most of them could not be found using 'Lafzi'; and you know the reason. It is questionable on why 'Lafzi' programmer and his supervisor to defend the use of 'Lafzi' even though they know they are wrong. Any correction and reprogramming of 'Lafzi' still does not work due to their lack of the basic knowledge of the Qoran.

From this booklet, the author is suggesting the 'Lafzi' programmer and his supervisor to voluntarily halt and retract 'Lafzi' from being used by the public prior to the comprehensive overhaul and prior to the approval of Departemen Agama RI. Personally, the author prays 'May Allah guide all of us especially in the correlation with the reciting, writing and practicing everything within the Qoran. Amin'.

The 'Lafzi' computer programmer and his supervisor are free to use all contents of this booklet for 'Lafzi' improvement if they have a chance; it is a small *sadaqah jariyah* for all Muslims.

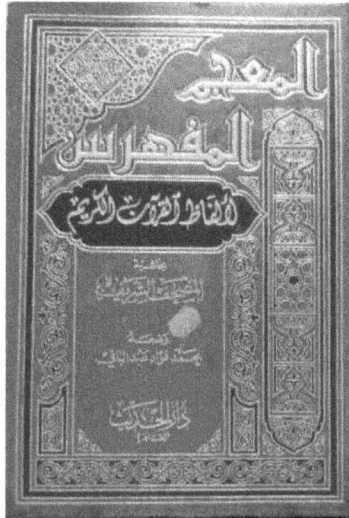

Index of the Qoran

8. THE INSTITUTIONAL APPROVAL

Institutional Approval

It is hard to believe if a famous University where the 'Lafzi' programmer and his supervisor have been studying, to approve 'Lafzi' computer application at http://apps.cs.ipb.ac.id/lafzi/web/. If it officially approved, it does mean some legal aspects may aply. It is right that it has a Computer Department but it does not have Department the Qoran Study. This University never taught the Qoran science and its relevant sciences; and its students never academically studied there about *isim muannaš, isim mauŝul, fi'lul-madhi, harfu-nafy, harfu-taukid, dhomir, tarkib idhofi, tarkib istišna, nahwu, sorf, balaghah* etc. which are became an integral part of the Qoran Study and correlate closely with the Qoran word (*lafz*) where 'Lafzi' is dealing with. A ridiculous example in 'Lafzi' computer application is about "**salat**" entry; the 'Lafzi' processed this input and based on the limited knowledge of the programmer and his supervisor, it displays the both correct and biased outputs: "**salat**", "ri**salat**", "t**salat**s", "al**lati**" etc.

The 'Lafzi' computer application is bearing the official name of the famous University/Institute in Indonesia. Is the 'Lafzi' a scientific presentation to meet the requirement to reach academic degree in the computer science at this Institute? If so, what is the responsibility of this University/Institute on the fundamental mistakes the 'Lafzi' made so far? Does this University approve 'Lafzi' computer application with all legal and moral responsibilities, both here in this world and the after life?

How does the entry of "inna salataka" come with so many serious mistakes? Here is the nightmare:

(1) The 'Lafzi' made 5 (five) mistakes relating to a single verse of Surah Al-Baqarah (2:228) over the search result of "**inna salataka**" phrase.

(2) The 'Lafzi' made 3 (three) mistakes relating to a single verse of Surah Al-Isra' (17:36) over the search result of "**inna salataka**" phrase.

(3) The 'Lafzi' made 1 (one) mistakes relating to a single verse of Surah An-Nisa' (4:103) over the search result of "**inna salataka**" phrase.

(4) The 'Lafzi' made 9 (nine) mistakes relating to a single verse of Surah Al-Ahqaaf (46:15) over the search result of "**inna salataka**" phrase.

(5) The 'Lafzi' made 1 (one) correct result and 1 (one) mistake relating to a single verse of Surah At-Taubah (9:103) over the search result of "**inna salataka**" phrase.

(6) The 'Lafzi' made 8 (eight) mistakes relating to a single verse of Surah Yusuf (12:31) over the search result of "**inna salataka**" phrase.

Altogether, 'Lafzi' made 1 only correct result plus 27 mistakes when searching "**inna salataka**" phrase. Where is its scientific value?

With one entry only, 'Lafzi' has made 27 mistakes, so how many more mistakes it is going to make for next 10, 100, 1000 entries? *Wallaahu a'lam*.

The ability (or inability or maybe disability) of 'Lafzi' to accept the entry based on the Indonesian pronunciation or *pelafalan* without typing the Arabic letter, has brought a very serious consequence since every single word of the Qoran is miracle, undisputable, inimitable, and *mu'jiz* which has the capability to crack and refute any challenge [Q2:23-24]. It is right that everybody has a freedom to create any computer application, but as it does have a potential to misguide the Muslims, and then the legal problem and liability may ensue.

The 'Lafzi' computer application to search the Qoran words within the URL http://apps.cs.ipb.ac.id/lafzi/web/ is a defective product; it is not scientific since it was not based on the Qoran science. Allah always protects the Qoran from anything bad [Q15:9]. It is not recommended to use this defective and confusing computer application until it gets fixed; it should have been fixed under the team of experts to avoid the liability and legal problem in the future. The Alma mater of 'Lafzi' programmer and his supervisor should have come forward to take this problem over.

The Department of Religious Affairs of the Republic of Indonesia has to scrutiny the 'Lafzi' computer application and to issue the decree to outlaw the 'Lafzi'. The *Lajnah Pentarjih/Pentas'hih Al-Qur'an Kemenag RI* has to certify the correctness of 'Lafzi' prior to its release to the public.

All mistakes –not the computer glitch–found within 'Lafzi' are NOT the Qoran's mistakes, the Qoran never be wrong, the programmer and his supervisor were.

A cover of the Qoran with a style

9. COMPUTER PROGRAMMING

Computer programming

It is not a computer glitch, it is the substantial mistake made by the 'Lafzi' programmer and his supervisor. The plausible explanation is the flawed algorithm which controls the flow of *input-process-output* of the computer. As an example, when the 'Lafzi' accepts the input or entry to search and find '**any word containing the letters of s, a, l, a, and t**' which has the meaning of 'prayer' and then the program keeps searching any word which contains the s-a-l-a-t letters even though the word does not have the meaning of 'prayer'. Why? Because the program does not have any information about the meaning and nomenclature of related word, the computer just keep searching and searching any word containing s-a-l-a-t letters. Why the program does not know that a certain word such as '**risalat**' even though it contains all letters of the entry but it does not have the meaning of 'prayer'? Why the 'Lafzi' does not know this very important information? Because the programmer does not know that! Why the 'Lafzi' programmer does not know that? Because he never learned the Qoran sciences. But why he did that? Because his supervisor does not know either, since he never learned the Qoran science. Why the supervisor does not know that? Because his Alma mater does not teach the Qoran science and does not have the Department of Qoran Science!

```
A  blind  person  wants  to  cross  the  super  busy
Sudirman  Boulevard  without  using  the  pedestrian
bridge.  Before  crossing  the  bridge,  he  needs
someone  to  help  him.  He  finds  the  other  blind
person. He asks 'Can you help me crossing this busy
boulevard with so many traffics?' 'Sure, I can.'
'How long are you blind?' 'Since 49 years ago, and
you?' 'Just  24  years  ago,  since  you  are  blind
longer, you must be better than me.' 'Yes, I am; I
have  a  good  tool,  a  white  stick'.  They  cross  the
busy  boulevard  and  at  the  same  time  the  *Batak
Angkot* Bus is passing by the point where they are
crossing.
```

It is a bitter parable, but that is the best one to describe the situation. The bridge has all safety requirements as described in [QS12:2, 16:103, 20:113, 26:195, 39:28, 41:3, 41:44, 42:7, 43:3, 46:12]. They do not know or do not care, what is the difference when it already happened?

The 'Lafzi' program keeps searching and searching any word bearing the letter of s-a-l-a-t even if the word is beyond the context of 'salat' (= prayer.) Since 'Lafzi' does not recognize the nomenclature of entry, and then it keeps searching eventhough the words of "riSALAT", "tSALATs", "alLATi", "arSALAT" etc. have nothing to do with "salat" or prayer.

The 'Lafzi' does not recognize that the entry of "salat" is within the classification of *isim nakirah mufrad muannaš;* it relies heavily on the Indonesian pronunciation while the Qoran is not the Indonesian pronunciation, it is Arabic pronunciation [Q12: 2]. This is *Lafzi*'s biggest mistake ever, since it was based on the wrong paradigm. Is there any verse that clearly states the Qoran pronounced in the Indonesian *pelafalan*? The 'Lafzi' keeps searching and considers the word of 'RISALAT' is within the classification of "salat" entry since it contains all letters of s-a-l-a-t, while 'RISALAT' (the last sounds T) does means the commands or divine guidance; and it is within the classification of *jamak muannaš salim nakirah* or the plural for masculine word of 'RISALAH' (the last sounds H). The smart 'Lafzi' keeps searching and finds the word of 'TSALATS' ثلاث which has a meaning of "three" but it meets the requirement as determined in the entry i.e. it has all letters of s-a-l-a-t, even though it has nothing to do with صلاة "salat".

How smart is it! The user wants to find 'salat' صلاة (= prayer), and 'Lafzi' finds "commands" (RISALAT), "three" (TSALATS), "which" (ALLATI), "sent" (ARSALAT) etc. since all of them have the common letters as specified in the entry "SALAT."

Good luck the lucky user of 'Lafzi'; you find the most weird computer programmer and his extraordinary supervisor! Congratulations to the Institute for having the distinctive student and supervisor who created 'Lafzi'!

The 'Lafzi' programmer and his supervisor knew the computer algorithm and computer programming but did not know the subject i.e. the Qoran words and the relative science where the 'Lafzi' is dealing with. It is better for them to design the 'Lafzi' alike to search and find the Latin '*lafaz*' within the Botany or anything else with the Indonesian pronunciation or '*pelafalan pembicara bahasa Indonesia*' which is **relevant** to their scientific discipline and Alma mater. The program could be named 'NGOCOLL' stands for <u>N</u>ew <u>G</u>eneration <u>of C</u>omputer <u>O</u>rientation for <u>L</u>atin <u>L</u>anguage to search and find the mystic names in botany to help the Indonesian peasants. Since they are the simple villagers they do not know the right '*pelafalan*' for entry. They type on the computer keyboard this entry "**cymbidium Hartinah ianum**", and suddenly the 'NGOCOLL' found every information relevant to the entry, even computer application makes a smart correction over the entry that there are 2 wrong spellings, you know, they are just the simple peasant. The other farmer put the entry of "**oryza sativa**", "**manihot walkerae**", and "***kurkuma santoriza***" one after another respectively. Wow, the NGOCOLL finds the valuable information and even it makes some corrections since the entry contains 5 wrong spellings altogether. It is still OK; they are just the simple peasants while the programmer and his supervisor are super experts.

To echoing the Qoran Surah Al-Baqarah: 23; the author is challenging the 'Lafzi' programmer and his supervisor for a national debate about the various mistakes of 'Lafzi'. If they lost, they have to discard the flawed 'Lafzi' and give their academic degrees up; and if the author lost he has to recall this booklet and give his academic degrees up. This is not a gambling, this is a responsibility to the truth, academic discipline and Allah. Do they agree or run away? *Wallahu a'lam.*

APPENDICES

1. Lampiran A, MUI

Yth. MUI;
Hal: Laporan bias ttg Al-Qur'an

Mohon dicoba aplikasi ini http://apps.cs.ipb.ac.id/lafzi/web/ dengan mengetik "salat", "sholat", atau "solat", hasilnya a.l. berupa RISALAT yang tidak berkaitan dengan "SALAT". Aplikasi yang berkaitan dengan Al-Qur'an ini jelas BIAS, dan mungkin sesat. Mohon selamatkan umat dari kesalahan aplikasi ini.
Mohon perhatian para Ulama. Terima kasih.

Abdul Rahman Bahry

email: abahry@hotmail.com
Cleveland, OH USA

2A. Lampiran B, email

Email dan komunikasi kepada ybs, setelah menggunakan aplikasi pada sekitar 13-14 Juli 2013, email pertama dikirim ke anggota milis Indonesian Muslim Society in America (IMSA):

2013/7/14 Abdul Rahman Bahry <abahry@hotmail.com>
Bismillaahirrahmaanirrahiim;

Subhanallah, in tengah Ramadhan yang penuh berkah ini kita dimanjakan dengan berbagai ni'mah a.l. keluarnya apps index Al-Qur'an (http://apps.cs.ipb.ac.id/lafzi/web/) yang sebelumnya harus kita cari in **Fathur-Rahman, Al-Mu'jamul-Mufahras,** atau **Index Cum-Concordance of Qur'an**. Cuma numpang saran, setelah dicoba apps atau link ke http://apps.cs.ipb.ac.id/lafzi/web/ hasilnya belum sepadan dengan ke tiga buku tersebut meskipun waktunya lebih cepat namun kurang cermat.
Berikut hasil uji coba dengan :

1. Ketika entri **Shalat**, atau **salat** dimasukkan untuk dicari, maka hasilnya ada beberapa lafadz in luar yang dimaksud yaitu salat atawa sembahyang, lalu
Hasil Pencarian (185 hasil), beberapa in antaranya tidak ada sangkut pautnya dengan salat, hanya dalam ejaan ada bunyi <u>salat</u> meskipun sebenarnya adalah ri_salat_. _Risalat_ bukan salat, salah satu contoh adalah dalam Surah Al-A'raf ayat 62 yang berarti "beberapa perintah" (dari Allah, yang juga meliputi beberapa perintah lain termasuk tauhid). Jadi hasil pencarian dengan entri "shalat" atau "salat" adalah bias.
Maksud pencarian kata atau entri "salat" atau "shalat" adalah satu *Isim nakirah mufrad muannas* yang berkonotasi dengan sembahyang/solat, namun hasilnya in samping benar merujuk ke sembahyang juga merujuk ke RISALAT yang sebenarnya secara lughat Qur'aniyyah adalah *Jamak mu'anats-Salim* dari mufrad/singular RISALAH.

Berikut beberapa BIAS yang lain:
رِسَالَٰتِ Surah Al-A'raf (7) ayat 62
رِسَالَٰتِ Surah Al-A'raf (7) ayat 68
رِسَالَٰتِ Surah Al-Jin (72) ayat 28

وَالْمُرْسَلَاتِ Surah Al-Mursalat (77) ayat 1

رِسَالَتَهُ Surah Al-An'am (6) ayat 124

2. صلاة ؟ Lalau bagaimana dengan entri menggunakan kata asli dalam Al-Qur'an

Hasil Pencarian (0 hasil)

Tidak ada hasil. Pastikan lafaz yang dicari adalah lafaz pada Al-Quran.

Ini komentar yang muncul in layar. Bagaimana ini? Dengan "salat" tidak kena semua dan dengan صلاة bahkan (0 hasil), benarkah tidak ada kata صلاة in dalam Al-Qur'an?

3. Hasil pencarian dengan entri "solat" bahkan membuahkan hasil yang lebih "mengerikan", pada hasil pencarian ke 32, 33, 35, 36 bahkan jauh sama sekali dari maksud semula.

3.1. Hasil #32
Surah An-Nahl (16) ayat 74

فَلَا تَضْرِبُوا

"**LA -T**adhribu dikategorikan "salat" karena mengandung bunyi "La T" yang sebenarnya berada in dua suku kata

3.2. Hasil #33
Surah Al-Mu'min (40) ayat 8

الَّتِي وَعَدْتَهُمْ

"ALLATII" adalah MAUSUL bukan ISIM MUFRAD MUANNATS sbagaimana kita masksud dengan salat; hanya karena mengandung bunyi "LAT" lalu menjadi salah satu hasil pencarian.

3.3. Hasil #35
Surah Al-Baqarah (2) ayat 196

وَلَا تَحْلِقُوا --- ثَلَاثَةِ

Hasil pencarian mengandung dua kesalahan, pertama pada **LA Tahliquu** (yang artinya JANGAN ENGKAU CUKUR), dan **TSALAATS (yang berarti TIGA)**, ini sangat serius. Pada kesalahan kedua bahkan tidak ada satu huruf hijai keempat "TS" yang dicari, kita mencari صلاة yang mengandung huruf Hijai ketiga (*koreksi: maksudnya keempat belas*) BUKAN KEEMPAT.

3.4. Hasil #36
Surah An-Nisa' (4) ayat 22

----- وَلَا تَنْكِحُوا

Mengandung dua kesalahan, bahkan pada hasil pencarian berikutnya semakin banyak kesalahan yang perlu kita perbaiki.

Insyaallah, sebelum apps ini diedarkan sebaiknya minta konfirmasi atau tas'hih Kementerian Agama karena menyangkut "penerbitan" yang ada kaitannya dengan Kitab Suci Al-Quran. Manakala penyusun apps atau website termaksud ini bekerja sama dengan seseorang atau sekelompok orang yang mengerti Bahasa Al-Qur'an termasuk Nahwu, Saraf, dan Balaghah insyallah hasilnya sama atau melebihi *Fathur-Rahman, Al-Mu'jamul-Mufahras,* atau *Index Cum-Concordance of Qur'an.*
Insyaallah, secara pribadi saya mendukung upaya mulia ini sekaligus perlu memberitahu teman-teman in Kemenag dan UIN agar waspada dengan bias yang mungkin timbul dari penggunaan
http://apps.cs.ipb.ac.id/lafzi/web/
Bagaimanapun, ini adalah usaha yang baik; semoga Allah menolong menyempurnakan kita semua. AD-DIINU NASHIIHAH. Amin.
[REDACTED] ▬▬▬▬▬▬▬▬▬▬▬▬▬▬▬▬▬▬▬▬

Terima kasih.

Abdul Rahman Bahry
Alumnus IAIN No. Ind. 374/AY
Cleveland, OH USA

2B. Lampiran C, respond

From: ridha@ipb.ac.id
Date: Mon, 15 Jul 2013 03:20:06 +0700
Subject: Re: BIAS http://apps.cs.ipb.ac.id/lafzi/web/

To: abahry@hotmail.com
CC: pinmas@kemenag.go.id; dumas@kemenag.go.id

Bismillahirrahmaanirrahiim,
Assalaamu'alaykum warahmatullahi wabarakaatuh,
[REDACTED, NEEDS PERMIT FROM SENDER]

3. Lampiran D, "inna salataka" entry

Penggunaan aplikasi http://apps.cs.ipb.ac.id/lafzi/web/ sekitar 16 Juli 2013 (susunan ayat mungkin berubah setelah disalin, harap dilihat pada hasil asli di komputer):

inna salataka

Hasil Pencarian (6 hasil)

☑ Tampilkan sorotan

1
Surah Al-Baqarah (2) ayat 228
39%
2
Surah Al-Isra' (17) ayat 36
38%
3
Surah An-Nisa' (4) ayat 103
37%
4
Surah Al-Ahqaaf (46) ayat 15
24%
5
Surah At-Taubah (9) ayat 103
22%
6
Surah Yusuf (12) ayat 31
19%

Pencarian dalam 0.01 detik

4. Lampiran E, "syahidnaa ala" entry

Penggunaan aplikasi http://apps.cs.ipb.ac.id/lafzi/web/ pada 18 Juli 2013 (susunan ayat mungkin berubah setelah disalin, harap dilihat pada hasil asli di komputer):

syahidnaa ala

Hasil Pencarian (2 hasil)

☑ Tampilkan sorotan

1
Surah Al-A'raf (7) ayat 172
66%
2
Surah Al-An'am (6) ayat 130
55%

Pencarian dalam 0.19 detik

KETERANGAN:
1. Al-A'raf (7) ayat 172, meskipun dalam ayat yang sama tetapi antara شَهِدْنَا dan عَلَى _terpisah
2. Al-An'am (6) ayat 130 شَهِدْنَا عَلَى lafadz "syahidna" yang langsung bersambung dengan "'ala" tidak disorot, malah "'ala" yang jauh terpisah dalam ayat yang sama yang disorot warna kuning.
   Kalau memang akan menampilkan شَهِدْنَا dan عَلَى secara terpisah maka seharusnya setiap ayat yang mengandung lafadz شَهِدْنَا juga harus ditampilkan. Misalnya شَهِدْنَا di:
3. Surah Yusuf (12) ayat 81 dan,
4. Surah An-Naml (27) ayat 49. Hal ini menunjukkan inkonsistensi aplikasi yang cenderung diskriminatif, bias dan meresahkan.

Sekiranya memang aplikasi ini akurat dan tidak bias, maka seharusnya hanya Surah Al-An'am (6) ayat 130 saja yang ditampilkan sebagai hasil karena entri inilah yang dimaksud untuk dicari secara khusus "syahidna ala", bukan "ala anfusihim ...." baru disambung dengan "syahidnaa" seperti dihasilkan dalam Al-A'raf (7) ayat 172.

The Popular Tafsir of Ibn Kašir

5. Lampiran F, "min rizq" entry

> min rizq

> Berikanlah masukan yang lebih panjang agar hasil lebih akurat.
> Pencarian dalam 0.03 detik

KETERANGAN:

Pencarian dengan dua suku kata "**min rizq**" gagal memperoleh hasil padahal setidaknya ada 3 (tiga) ayat yang persis mengandung bunyi atau pelafalan "min rizq"; pertama in Surah Al-Baqarah (2) ayat 60, kedua in Surah Yunus (11) ayat 59, dan ketiga Surah Saba' (34) ayat 15 tetapi tidak satupun ditampilkan. in Surah Al-A'raf (7) ayat 32 ada kemiripan bunyi "min rizq" yaitu "min (ar) riqz" tetapi tidak ditampilkan sebagai hasil. Sementara itu pencarian lafadz "**min ar rizq**" menghasilkan tampilan Surah Al-Baqarah (2) ayat 233; padahal di dalam ayat ini tidak ada lafadz "min ar rizq", lafadz yang ada adalah "**rizquhunna**" رِزْقُهُنَّ sekiranya hasil "**rizq**uhunna" dapat dapat diterima sebagai bagian dari "min ar **rizq**", maka seharusnya ayat-ayat yang mengandung bunyi atau pelafalan "**rizq**" harus konsisten ditampilkan semua bukan hanya in Q2:233 saja.

Lafadz yang berbunyi **rizq** dan derivatifnya di seluruh Al-Qur'an jumlahnya ada 123 yang hanya dapat diketahui melalui **_Ilmu-Sharf_** padahal ilmu dahsyat yang menjadi dasar pengetahuan tentang lafadz Al-Qur'an ini di luar disiplin dan kapasitas akademik penyusun dan pembimbing aplikasi termaksud. Dengan demikian alasan dan jawaban Sdr. sebagaimana disampaikan melalui email (Lampiran 2) kurang tepat dan harus ditolak. Bagaimana menerangkan adanya puluhan lafadz "rizq" di dalam Al-Qur'an yang tidak dapat dihasilkan dengan menggunakan aplikasi yang kacau ini?

Kita tidak apriori terhadap aplikasi ini khusunya keberhasilan menampilkan satu atau dua ayat yang kita cari dengan tepat, tetapi kesalahannya jauh lebih banyak, kita tidak dapat menggunakan dan menerapkan kaidah *Ushul-Fiqh* "Akhoffudh-dhororoini" ataupun *alasan syar'ie* lainnya yang dapat membenarkan dan mendukung aplikasi http://apps.cs.ipb.ac.id/lafzi/web/ ini berhubung *madhorot* atau bahayanya jauh lebih banyak dari manfaatnya. Aplikasi ini jelas-jelas tidak akurat dan menyesatkan.

6. Lampiran G, "al kalalah" entry

al kalalah

Hasil Pencarian (13 hasil)

☑ Tampilkan sorotan

1
Surah Al-Maidah (5) ayat 97
41%
2
Surah Al-An'am (6) ayat 77
40%
3
Surah Al-Maidah (5) ayat 2
37%
4
Surah Yunus (10) ayat 81
35%
5
Surah Ali-'Imran (3) ayat 159
33%
6
Surah Az-Zumar (39) ayat 71
25%
7
Surah Ar-Rum (30) ayat 30
19%
8
Surah Al-A'raf (7) ayat 50
19%
9
Surah An-Nisa' (4) ayat 141
19%
10
Surah Yunus (10) ayat 5
17%
11
Surah Al-A'raf (7) ayat 54

17%
12
Surah An-Nisa' (4) ayat 171
2%
13
Surah Al-Baqarah (2) ayat 286
1%
Halaman :

Pencarian dalam 0.01 detik

KETERANGAN:
Pencarian lafadz **"al kalalah"** menghasilkan sesuatu yang akan secara definitif menuntun kita untuk segera melarang aplikasi http://apps.cs.ipb.ac.id/lafzi/web/. Hanya ada dua **"al kalalah"** in dalam seluruh Al-Quran; pertama in Surah An-Nisa' (4) ayat 12, dan kedua in Surah An-Nisa' (4) ayat 176 tetapi gagal ditampilkan semua, bahkan aplikasi ini "ngaco" dan melenceng ke 13 hasil pencarian yang semuanya salah seperti ditampilkan in atas.

[A part of Appendix to Secretary of Religious Affairs, Republic of Indonesia is REDACTED]

Mohon dengan hormat aplikasi http://www.cs.ipb.ac.id/lafzi/web/ dinyatakan resmi dan menyesatkan serta dilarang in seluruh wilayah RI demi kemaslahatan umat Islam dan demi mencegah hal-hal yang tidak kita inginkan in kemudian hari. Terima kasih.

42

7. Most Recent Result

In April 2014, the existing 'Lafzi' with a facelift is on action to search some 'lafaz' or words. Alhamdu lillah, it is a little bit better, but is still without approval from Department of Religious Affairs of the Republic of Indonesia to use in Indonesia jurisdiction.

Note:
In this booklet, some verses are not fully quoted or displayed; they were fully displayed in 'Lafzi'. Please refer to the original text of the Qoran for more accuracy.

Ketikkan lafaz

☑ Perhitungkan huruf vokal

Ketikkan potongan ayat atau lafaz dalam Al-Quran (tidak harus benar cara penulisannya), contoh:

- alhamdulillahi rabbil-'alamin

- innalloha ma'a shoobiriin

- laa ilaaha illallaah

- kun fayakuun

Tips: Gunakan spasi untuk pemisah antar-kata agar lebih akurat.

alhamdulillahi ı

Hasil Pencarian (2 hasil)

☑ Tampilkan terjemahan   ☑ Tampilkan sorotan

1
Surat Al-Fatihah (1) ayat 2
100%
الْحَمْدُ لِلَّهِ رَبِّ الْعَالَمِينَ
2
Surat Al-Mu'min (40) ayat 65
92%

Pencarian dalam 0.34 detik

---

innalloha ma'a

Hasil Pencarian (3 hasil)

☑ Tampilkan terjemahan ☑ Tampilkan sorotan

1
Surat Al-Anfal (8) ayat 46
100%
2
Surat Al-Baqarah (2) ayat 153
100%
3
Surat Al-Baqarah (2) ayat 249
76%

Pencarian dalam 0.07 detik

---

laa ilaaha illalla

44

Hasil Pencarian (5 hasil)

☑ Tampilkan terjemahan ☑ Tampilkan sorotan

1
Surat An-Nisa' (4) ayat 171
100%
2
Surat At-Taghabun (64) ayat 13
100%
3
Surat Ash-Shaffat (37) ayat 35
100%
4
Surat Muhammad (47) ayat 19
100%
5
Surat Al-Mu'minun (23) ayat 116
83%
Pencarian dalam 0.07 detik

kun fayakuun

Hasil Pencarian (9 hasil)

☑ Tampilkan terjemahan ☑ Tampilkan sorotan

1
Surat Al-Baqarah (2) ayat 117
100%
2
Surat Ali-'Imran (3) ayat 47
100%

3
Surat Ali-'Imran (3) ayat 59
100%
4
Surat Al-An'am (6) ayat 73
100%
5
Surat An-Nahl (16) ayat 40
100%
6
Surat Maryam (19) ayat 35
100%
7
Surat Al-Furqan (25) ayat 7
100%
8
Surat Yasin (36) ayat 82
100%
9
Surat Al-Mu'min (40) ayat 68
100%

Pencarian dalam 0.06 detik

The entry other than suggested by the programmer to test the accuracy of 'Lafzi':

w a hiya dukh

Hasil Pencarian (1 hasil)

☑ Tampilkan terjemahan ☑ Tampilkan sorotan

1
Surat Fushshilat (41) ayat 11
100%

Pencarian dalam 0.03 detik

jahidil kuffara

Hasil Pencarian (2 hasil)

☑ Tampilkan terjemahan ☑ Tampilkan sorotan

1
Surat At-Taubah (9) ayat 73
100%
2
Surat Al-Tahrim (66) ayat 9
100%
Pencarian dalam 0.03 detik

li kulli nabain n

Hasil Pencarian (0 hasil) ??

Tidak ada hasil. Pastikan lafaz yang dicari adalah lafaz pada Al-Quran.

li kulli naba'in r

Hasil Pencarian (1 hasil)

☑ Tampilkan terjemahan ☑ Tampilkan sorotan

1
Surat Al-An'am (6) ayat 67
100%

Pencarian dalam 0.03 detik

> kaf ha ya ain ‹

Hasil Pencarian (1 hasil)

☑ Tampilkan terjemahan ☑ Tampilkan sorotan

1
Surat Maryam (19) ayat 1
100%

Pencarian dalam 0.03 detik

> alif lam mim ta₁

Hasil Pencarian (0 hasil) ??

Tidak ada hasil. Pastikan lafaz yang dicari adalah lafaz pada Al-Quran.

> alif lam mim

Hasil Pencarian (8 hasil)

☑ Tampilkan terjemahan ☑ Tampilkan sorotan

1
Surat Al-Baqarah (2) ayat 1
100%
2
Surat Ali-'Imran (3) ayat 1
100%
3
Surat Al-A'raf (7) ayat 1
100%
4
Surat Ar-Ra'd (13) ayat 1
100%
5
Surat Al-'Ankabut (29) ayat 1
100%
6
Surat Ar-Rum (30) ayat 1
100%
7
Surat Luqman (31) ayat 1
100%
8
Surat As-Sajdah (32) ayat 1
100%

Pencarian dalam 0.03 detik

Author's other books are available also at createspace.com and
amazon.com

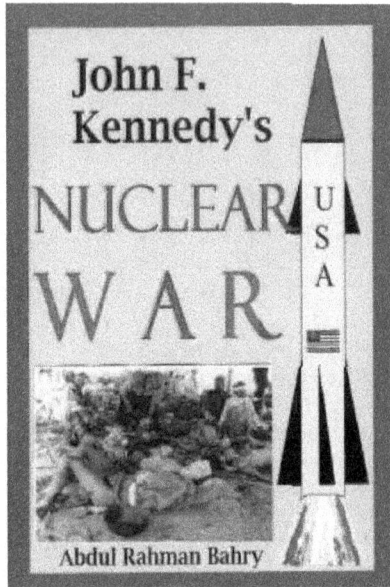

John F.
Kennedy's

NUCLEAR

W A R

U
S
A

Abdul Rahman Bahry

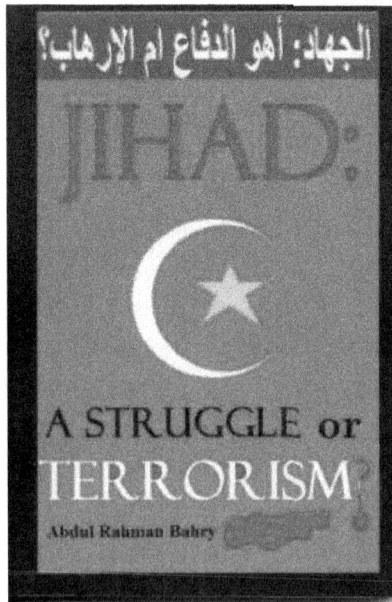

الجهاد: أهو الدفاع ام الإرهاب؟

JIHAD:

A STRUGGLE or
TERRORISM?

Abdul Rahman Bahry

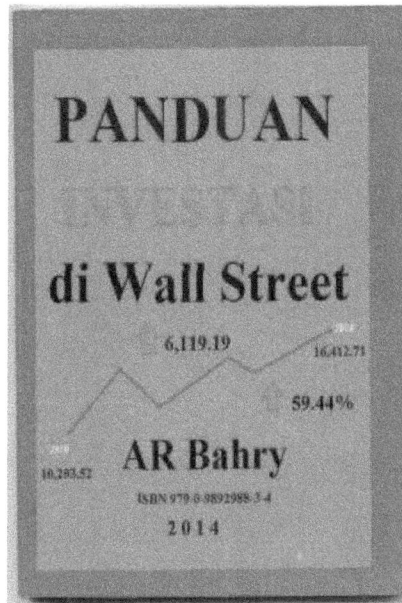

PANDUAN

INVESTASI

di Wall Street

6,119.19

16,412.71

59.44%

AR Bahry

ISBN 970-0-9892988-3-4

2 0 1 4

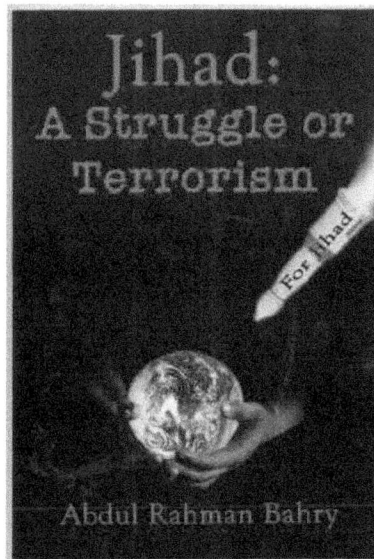

Jihad:
A Struggle or Terrorism

For Jihad

Abdul Rahman Bahry

www.ingramcontent.com/pod-product-compliance
Lightning Source LLC
Chambersburg PA
CBHW071738020426

42331CB00008B/2081